THE
Archive Photographs
SERIES

TENBURY WELLS
AND THE TEME VALLEY

Tenbury Board of Guardians, 1930. This was their last meeting as the Workhouse system was ending. Top: D.J. Morris (Relieving Officer), G.V. Searle (Work House Master), G. Meredith (Whitton). Middle row: H.T. Knott (Tenbury), F. Lucas (D. Clerk), L. Ashley (Clerk), R. Crofts (Knighton), B. Jenkins (Bockleton), F. Rawlings (Greete), W.G. Maund (Rochford), G. Haywood (Tenbury). Front row: Col R.H. Wingfield-Cardiff (Little Hereford), J.W. Rose (Burford), Col. E.V. Wheeler (Tenbury), Revd E.E. Lea (Eastham), Wm Baldwin (Boraston), Sir Charles Rushout (Burford), C.G. Partridge (Lindridge).

THE
Archive Photographs
SERIES

TENBURY WELLS
AND THE TEME VALLEY

Compiled by
Howard Miller

CHALFORD

First published 1996
Copyright © Howard Miller, 1996

The Chalford Publishing Company
St Mary's Mill, Chalford,
Stroud, Gloucestershire, GL6 8NX

ISBN 0 7524 0722 8

Typesetting and origination by
The Chalford Publishing Company
Printed in Great Britain by
Redwood Books, Trowbridge

Acknowledgements

I would like to thank the following for the loan of photographs
and, also, for their help in identifying pictures.
I apologise in advance if I have missed anyone out.
People have been marvellous in supplying old photographs
so that, in the end, I could choose which ones to use:
Mary Coles, the Bowketts, Mary Thorpe, G.H. Kendrick,
J.G. Banfield and Sons, Doug Powis, Tenbury Museum, A.B. Demauss,
Norton Barracks, Record Office (Spetchley), the Town Council,
Tenbury Historical Society, D. Spilsbury, C. Norman, Mary Rudd,
Tom Higginson, Steve Giles, Dot James,
Burford House and Richard Lloyd Ltd.

Contents

Acknowledgements   4

Foreword   6

Introduction   7

1.   Teme Street, Tenbury   9

2.   Streets off the Market Place   27

3.   Around the District   51

4.   Rivers   73

5.   Sport and Recreation   83

6.   Special Occasions   105

7.   People at Work   115

Foreword

The nineteenth century saw changes to Tenbury as industrialisation and so transport got into full swing. The canal came through Tenbury, although as it did not reach Stourport it failed to pay for itself. Tenbury Improvement Society was formed, the railway came through Tenbury and the Spa was built, which led to the renaming of Tenbury to Tenbury Wells. The Corn Exchange and Round Market were built to benefit from the improved transport.

This book tries to tell some of this recent history in photographs. The camera has recorded for us the pictures of its changing buildings, its people at work and play and tries to show how Tenbury became the interesting and picturesque market town it is today.

Margaret Morris
Mayor of Tenbury Wells
Council Offices
Tenbury Wells

Introduction

Tenbury – the name derives from Temebury, meaning the fort on the Teme – is an ancient town at an important river crossing. It was said that in 1615 it was the main thoroughfare for trade between Wales and London. The main street used to be Church Street and the wide triangular market area can still be seen by the Round Market. Tenbury had its market status granted in 1248 and it was soon after that date that the Teme Bridge was built and the Burgage plots of Teme Street laid out. It has remained the same since then.

In the nineteenth century, Tenbury, for administration purposes, was divided into four hamlets: Tenbury Town, Tenbury Foreign, Sutton and Berrington. The River Teme is also the county boundary dividing Shropshire on the north, from Worcestershire on the south. On the south of Tenbury flows the Kyre, joining up with the Teme on the east of the town. Tenbury has been subject to flooding over the years and seems to have had one particularly bad flood every century: in 1615 when the bridge was destroyed, in 1770 when the church was destroyed and in 1886 when the water came up to the ceilings of some houses and one person was killed. Nowadays however, the river authorities seem to have solved the problem of diverting the water.

It seems appropriate to introduce Tenbury, not as it is now, but as it was in the first decade of this century, the time from which most of these photographs come. This is a tourist's introduction to the region in the year 1910:

'Lying on a branch line of the Great Western Railway the small town of Tenbury – often confused with Tenby or Tetbury – is to many folk hardly known even by name. A few musical folk know of its College of St Michael, a few fishermen come for trout or grayling, a few cyclists and motorists halt here; but by the ordinary holidaymaker it is quite untouched. Yet it is a centre of rare beauty, and has much to attract those who love not the places where tourists herd.

The journey from London – the best trains take three and a half hours – is by a picturesque route up the Thames Valley, past the spires and domes of Oxford, through the high Cotswold plain, by the plum orchards of Evesham and Pershore, past Worcester and its cathedral, by the oak-clad hills of the Wyre Forest and the brawling little River Rea, into the wide Teme Valley where Tenbury lies. At Tenbury three counties meet. The town is in Worcestershire, the station in Shropshire, and a mile further up the Teme, Herefordshire begins.

It is a country of uncommon richness; orchards of apple, plum, pear and cherry and hopyards with long over-arched avenues like church aisles lie in the valley and ascend its slopes. The region is at its loveliest in April and May, when the orchards are a sea of white and pink blossom, but in September and October, the time of fruit gathering, hop picking and cider making, it has a charm of luscious ripeness.

Tenbury lies between two rivers, the Teme and its little tributary, the Kyre. Entering the place from the station, you cross the swirling Teme over a mediaeval bridge – sadly spoiled by a recent widening – and pass up the broad main street. Then at a right angle comes the narrow curving Market Street, with the Kyre flowing beside it, and you are soon at the round, red Butter Cross in the Market Square. Thence on one side a road leads to the church, on the other, quiet, sleepy Cross Street brings you to the end of the town. It is but a little place: the population is only fourteen hundred. A good deal of mellow eighteenth century brick remains, and some typical black and white houses, notably four old inns, the Royal Oak, the King's Head, The Hop Pole (now named Pembroke House), and across the river, the Rose and Crown.

The town has an asset which might be far more developed than it has been, a spring of saline waters, highly recommended by doctors for heart trouble and rheumatism. Though a pump room and baths exist, they have been closed by the owner. A man of money and enterprise, it is probable, might make Tenbury another Cheltenham or Droitwich. Meanwhile it remains a little, quiet market town in the midst of its orchards.'

Finally, in a book such as this, there are bound to be some errors in naming people or objects as the information relies mainly on peoples' memories. No doubt you will inform me of these errors so that I can correct them. All the photographs that have been presented to me I shall pass on to the Tenbury Museum for safe keeping.

One
Teme Street, Tenbury

This has been the main street of the town since the thirteenth century and is still laid out in its original Burgage plots.

A Victorian view
of Tenbury's
Pump Rooms

The Pump Rooms, as laid out in their heyday with timber cladding and a single-storey attendant's cottage. Various accommodation was provided for visitors and the streets were paved so that they could promenade and keep clean. Unfortunately, the expected influx of visitors never took place and it has had a struggle to survive.

Teme Street in 1897. Here the Diamond Jubilee celebrations in Teme Street are seen in a view looking towards the Court. Queen Victoria celebrated sixty years on the throne during 1897. Evident in the advertising on the right are C. Musselwhite, Royal Enfield Bicycles (with a cycle above the shop), Tobacco and Dancer's Boots. You can see the police station on the left, with its official notices. Musselwhite's had an 'outfitting establishment' with clothes from London houses of the best repute. Of course there were separate rooms for ready made clothes.

Teme Street in flood in 1901. Teme Street flooded from the north with the River Teme and from the south with the River Kyre. The floods were an obvious tourist attraction requiring the presence of two constables. The River Kyre was the start of the flooding when it rose. The Teme then rose, preventing the Kyre waters from dispersing. This caused backflooding in Market Street, which was the first thoroughfare to suffer from the high waters.

Teme Street in flood in 1924, looking from the bridge towards the Court which can be seen in the distance. This was another year of great floods and damage to stock held in cellars.

Teme Street in 1903. Mr E. Howard is facing the camera on the road. On the left can be seen one of the workhouse inmates working at a pile of stones. The Bridge Hotel on the right looks very different without its black and white façade.

Teme Street in 1946. This is a view of post-war Tenbury with an Austin Seven, Morris Eight and a Morris Ten Series M seen coming towards us. On the left is a Bedford van belonging to K.A. Long, Motorfactors, Worcester.

Lloyds Bank in 1930. The left hand Bank house has now been demolished. In the 1880s it was said of the design, 'Tenbury branch has come out in quite a new decorative character. The painting is of the Pompeian order suggested by the architect, Mr Curzon. The residents of Tenbury ought to feel grateful to the managers and Mr Curzon for introducing this style, which is conspicuous by its surroundings, but must be considered by people of taste a most pleasing feature.'

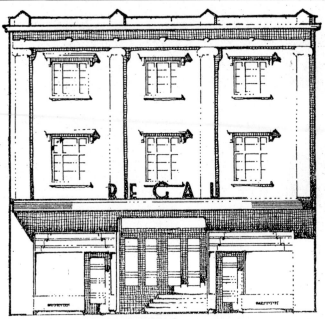

WORCESTERSHIRE'S NEW LUXURY CINEMA,

REGAL

PHONE 100   **TENBURY WELLS.**   PHONE 100

Grand Opening Thursday, July 29th, at 7-30 p.m.

CICELY COURTNEIDGE AND ERNEST TREUX
—in—

Everybody Dance

LAUREL AND HARDY
—in—

THEM THAR HILLS

COLOUR CARTOON.——GOOD LITTLE MONKEYS.

THE REGAL is air conditioned for your health and comfort and not just ventilated; the only plant of its kind within a radius of 20 miles.

PROGRAMME commences—Monday, Wednesday, Thursday and Friday at 7-30. Tuesday 2 p.m. and 7-30. Saturday and Bank Holidays 2-30, continuous from 5-30.

FREE CYCLE PARK at rear of Theatre. Earphones for the deaf. Free Car Park at Messrs. Edwards, Russell and Baldwin's Parking Ground, near Theatre.

Prices of Admission :—

Balcony 1/6; Stalls 1/3; Centre Stalls 1/-Front Stalls 6d.
BARGAIN MATINEES AND REDUCED PRICES FOR CHILDREN.
Monthly Programmes posted to patrons leaving name and address at Box Office.

New Cinema, 1937. The cinema was moved from the Corn Exchange where it had been since 1917. The Regal was a purpose-built cinema with air conditioning.

Ironmonger's shop, 1905. James Gay Banfield is in the doorway of his shop which he had bought from Mrs Pountney in 1864. They are still trading as ironmongers and must be the oldest retail business in Tenbury. They were quite innovative in the early 1900s as they started a garage business and were the first electrical retailers in the community.

The rear of the Corn Exchange in 1954. This was built in 1862 when it was thought that there would be a big expansion of business due to the coming of the railway. This back-end has now been replaced by a single-storey extension. It can be seen that the architect, Mr Cranston, was used to modernising churches. The Corn Exchange would have been equally at home as a chapel.

G.E.T.H. Maund's petrol station, Teme Street, in 1954. Mr Maund started a garage business in Rochford in 1924 as an Austin agent before moving to Teme Street.

Maund's, c. 1950, showing a 1913 Rolls-Royce Silver Ghost which had been on the coachbuilder's stand at the 1913 Motor Show. It was in Maund's garage for minor repairs.

16

Price the Saddler, 1890. Charles Price stands in his doorway with his stock. He built up a good business at No. 8 Teme Street but died in 1894. Mrs Price brought in Tom Downes from Cleobury to manage the business. By 1898, T.H. Downes had taken over and ran it until 1916.

Saddlers, No. 45 Teme Street, in 1954. A.W.D. Gore, affectionately known as 'Old Farf', died in 1955 aged 80. At 12 he was apprenticed to the firm of saddlers, T. Price Ltd, and he also used to deliver telegrams for the Post Office. He took over the saddlery business from Mr Downes and worked there until his death. He was widely known in hockey circles for being a full back with Harry Higgins. Among the hockey players he was known as 'Old Whiskers' and played until well past the age of 50. He used to fox and otter hunt and he had a formidable reputation in cycle races. Known as 'Superman', he was also the undisputed champion of sack races. No one ever caught him.

ESTABLISHED 1849.

Goodall & Sons,

Family Grocers,
TEA DEALERS,
WINE AND SPIRIT MERCHANTS,
ITALIAN WAREHOUSEMEN,
BAKERS AND CONFECTIONERS.

TENBURY.

Goodall's in 1890. Benjamin Goodall had these two buildings put up in Teme Street in the 1880s. The top one is now Spencer's, the bakers, on the east side; the bottom one is opposite and contains the licensed premises, The Vaults.

Candle Factory in 1954. This is an unusual building behind the shops on the west side of Teme Street. Once a three-storey factory, it has now been reduced to two storeys. It was known as a Candle and Sailmaking Factory. There used to be tallow chandlers in Tenbury and the factory probably supplied their needs.

Flooding in Teme Street in 1924. One of the shops reported that the cellars were full and the water was two feet above the cellar level. The houses on the right have now made way for a supermarket. The mound in the background is the Yew Tree which used to be in the grounds of the Swan Hotel.

Middleton's corner shop in 1875. Later on, at the turn of the century, it became known as Gardner's corner shop. The boy is Mr W. Middleton and he is seen here with his aunt. Mr W. Middleton became a parish councillor and was a well known postman.

The top of Teme Street in 1910 showing Gardner's Central Bazaar displaying a full range of goods. Next door is the barbers and its pole. Notice how the scaffolding poles were put in beer barrels painted white – an effective safety device for pedestrians.

Teme Street in 1920 from Gardner's Corner looking towards the bridge. A steam engine would not be doing the road surface much good and, opposite, a car is being filled up with petrol on the roadside, at Banfield's garage.

Teme Street in 1905. The small stone spread on the top surface can clearly be seen. It was left to the wagons to roll it in. Part of the task of workhouse people was to break up Clee Hill stone for road mending. The Crow on the right has changed considerably. There wasn't much space at this corner, especially when the old Town Hall was on the corner opposite Gardner's. It left only 11 ft 6 in of road space. In 1883 an oak tree on two timber carriages and drawn by eleven horses, passed through Tenbury from Kyre to Hereford. The tree was 80 ft long and had great difficulty in negotiating this corner.

Teme Street in 1897. The occasion is that of the Diamond Jubilee of the reign of Queen Victoria. The street through which the procession is due to pass is being swept. 'The bell ringers ascended the tower and rang some merry peals. The Tenbury Volunteer band played a selection of music in the Market Square.'

Action in Teme Street in 1905. The gentleman in the centre seems to be catching something falling – a child or a dog? All eyes are on the incident.

Teme Street, *c.* 1910, showing a busy street scene looking north towards the river. C. Price the saddler is the first shop on the right. John Jukes, on the left, opened a draper's shop in 1908, known as The White Shop.

No 8 Teme Street, *c.* 1920. On the right is Palmer's, the jewellers, whose wife gave piano lessons. There is a notice in the window saying 'Opera House, Bus Service'. Next door is No. 8 which was Barclays Bank from 1919 to 1924 and next again is Goodall and Sons, who had this house built in about 1890. Finally, we see Frank Bloom's clothing warehouse.

The Pump Rooms, *c.* 1905. These were built in 1862 at the rear of The Crow Hotel by the Tenbury Improvement Company, after trying several sites: one opposite The Swan Hotel and another along the Berrington Lane. It was hoped that the discovery of mineral water and the coming of the railway would make the town another Cheltenham.

Bridge Cottage, *c.* 1905. The building to the left has now been demolished. It is hard to understand why this cottage was built so low down near the river as it must have been constantly flooded. A Thomas Mantle lived here. His occupation was coal carving and he tried to present Princess Victoria with some of his work when she passed by on the way to Witley Court in 1832. Unfortunately, he dropped the gifts going over the Teme Bridge, but the Princess heard about it and presented him with an address.

The Court in 1966 in the process of being demolished to make way for a housing estate. This was the home of the Godson family, starting with Septimus Holmes Godson who found mineral water near the Court and started the drive towards changing Tenbury into Tenbury Wells.

The Court, again in 1966. This is the view of the Court as it appeared from Teme Street. It was along to the right that the first mineral water well was discovered, and rediscovered by the demolition men, who quickly filled it with concrete.

Kyrewood House in 1917. This was the home of the Wheeler family who were solicitors and influential people in Tenbury. They eventually moved to Newnham Court. The house has a classical Georgian north elevation with a fine domed and galleried hall. Here, wounded British soldiers are seen relaxing at the back of Kyrewood House which was handed over for use as a convalescent home during the the First World War.

Two
Streets off Market Place

Having gone up Teme Street we can deal with the rest of historic Tenbury, which includes three more streets: Market, Church and Cross.

The Royal Oak in 1882. This is an older photograph of the Royal Oak, a seventeenth-century hotel which, during the time that most of these photographs were taken, was managed by Sam Mattock, who has the distinction of having started a bowling club in Tenbury. The photograph also shows the state of the roads. This one has had a fresh dressing of small stones. The shop on the left was owned by A. Jeff (milliner), who was having a sale.

The Royal Oak, c. 1920. Pubs then used to provide breakfast at 1s 6d for a round of gammon, two eggs, tea and as much bread as you wanted. Roast dinners were 2s. Pubs also used to organise outings for which you paid 6d per week plus 10s on the day. You had bread, cheese and pickle as a snack. Ham and beef were brought and carved for lunch and you went to a pub for a cooked meal. A 'gentleman' used to get off the train, walk to the Oak, sit on the top step and commence to play the harp; after collecting enough money off he would go.

Barwise Shop, Market Street in 1910. Barbara Barwise is standing in the doorway. She was a dress and costume maker and her mother purchased the business from Miss Whatnough in 1906. The house was demolished to give the Royal Oak parking space at the front.

Market Street in flood in 1901. The Kyre runs along Market Street on the south side. Mr Baverstock, clerk to the Godson estate, rowed a boat along Market Street during this flood.

Market Street in 1902. The clock on the Clock House has written around it 'Use time wisely'. Joseph Hellaby took over the business in 1892 and traded as The Clock House Supply Stores.

The Butter Market in 1903. The Butter Market, built in 1858, replaced an earlier structure built in 1811. John Jeff, shown on the left, remembered the old Butter Cross which was an open plan structure on six pillars and was a cold and miserable place in winter. Jeff was Clerk to the Parish Council and worked for Norris and Miles for sixty years. In 1858 he walked to Kidderminster to catch a train to Birmingham to see Queen Victoria. He was often up at 4.00 am, walked five or six miles to meet the hunt, but was always in his office by 10.00 am. The other gentleman is Mr A. Handley.

The Butter Market in 1920. Vehicles are starting to appear but there are no traffic jams. The Butter Market is usually referred to as the Round Market even though it is oval in shape.

The Round Market in 1925 in a view looking down Church Street with the church in the background. This triangular area used to be the old market place of the town. The notices announce weekly auctions on Tuesdays, as still happens today.

A pair of posh prams outside the Royal Oak in 1920. Perhaps their owners are waiting for husbands to appear from the Royal Oak.

The May Fair in 1920 in the Market Square. There were stalls all down Church Street. The horse-drawn fair wagons still wait to be unloaded. This fair is a relic of the Market Charter of 1248 when the Lord of the Manor collected rent from the stall-holders. There were galloping horses, hoop-la, shooting galleries, coconut shies, hammer-punching machines and swings. However people were starting to get fed up with the fairs on the streets and there were calls for them to be moved to the Palmers.

Market Street in 1901 during the severe floods of that year. The notice saying 'Fish Cheap' is a bit ironic. Next door is The Hole in the Wall and then Gardner's, the watch and clock maker.

Bank Chambers in 1900 looking down Church Street. The brass plate proclaims 'Berwick Lechmere Worcester Old Bank'. The Chambers were known as Holland House, as Samuel Holland built them in the late eighteenth century. He was so influential that Church Street was known as All Holland Street during the nineteenth century.

Tenbury Church in 1903. The church of St Mary's was much damaged by floods in 1770 but the Norman tower remained intact. It seems strange building a church so near the river, but 400 or 500 years ago the river ran in a loop to near the Rose and Crown. It may have been during the great floods of 1615, which destroyed the bridge, that the river found its present course.

Interior of Tenbury Church in 1906. The north aisle (left) was probably the chantry formed to pray for the soul of Roger de Osborn in 1290. The south aisle contains the Acton Tomb and can be seen on the east wall. The church had a major refurbishment in 1864 when the box pews, which could be bought at 12s 6d per annum per seat, were replaced by these free seats.

Tenbury Church in 1900; the interior is decorated for Easter. The rather large font cover is now in Tenbury Museum. The east end of the north aisle had an organ installed in the 1890s, hence the doorway and three light window above. At Candlemas, figures of the Virgin Mary were removed and snowdrops (Christ's flowers) were scattered in their place. It was considered unlucky to pick them for any other purpose. Some still grow by the Church House.

Acton Tomb in 1906. Thomas Acton of Sutton, who died in 1546, had three children, two sons who died young and a daughter, Joyce. She was betrothed to Sir Thomas Lucy at the age of twelve. It was their deer that Shakespeare is alleged to have shot.

Church Street Cottages in 1860. These half-timbered cottages of the seventeenth century have now been demolished. The sign over one door says 'fireman'; this cottage housed one of the volunteer fire brigade on call to use the fire engine housed in the Engine House near the church (now a parish room). Note the bread delivery boy.

The Old Vicarage in 1835. These are window tiles from the old Rectory, now a nursing home. The tile on the left is broken. The house on the right is the old Rectory with, next door, the Great House built by the last Baron of Burford, Francis Cornewall. Its gardens used to stretch to the back of the Royal Oak. It is said that the bricks from the Great House were used to build Berrington House. Both buildings were knocked down by the Revd G. Hall in 1838 so that he could build the more grand Rectory which is the present nursing home.

The Market Square in 1880. There were four shops as well as the Market Tavern in this triangle. The shop on the left was an ironmonger's. They were all pulled down soon after this photograph was taken as they were considered a slum area of Tenbury. This included the Market Tavern but this was rebuilt as the present public house. The Round Market, which had been built for twenty years, can be seen on the left.

Cross Street in 1910. There was plenty of time to stand in the road and debate the politics of the day as there was very little traffic about. The notice outside the shop reads 'Coal, Lime, Salt, Bricks, Tiles, Pipes'.

Cross Street in 1905. This is an unusual view of the King's Head taken from the entrance to old Trumpet Yard. Dale, Forty & Co. enthusiastically advertised their pianos as there was also a similar notice outside the Rose and Crown. The house behind the donkey is Stafford House, named after William Strafford [sic].

Cross Street in 1905, this time looking towards the Round Market. Stafford House is on the left and there have now been rather a lot of alterations on the right. The King's Head sign shows up just above the horse and cart.

Norville House, seen here in 1905, was built in the 1850s using the same brick and stone as for St Michael's church. It looks as though it was the same architect as well. Captain Avery bought the house with the intention of founding a Catholic church and services were held in the stable block at the rear. Finally the house was pulled down and the Catholic church built in its grounds. In the 1880s Norville House was a ladies school run by Miss Slade who 'receives young ladies to board and educate on moderate terms'.

A wagon outside the King's Head in 1932. No drinking and driving! The Thornycroft wagon (GC 9039) belonged to the LMR/GWR railway company and replaced the horse-drawn dray on 1 February 1930. The first driver of this lorry was Reuben Martin. It is standing outside the King's Head in Cross Street, with the Round Market visible at the bottom of the street.

Pembroke Lodge in 1905. This used to be the toll-house for the Tenbury Turnpike Trust with two gates, one for Bromyard Road and the other for the Oldwood Road. Lime from Knowbury was allowed through the gates free of toll as the landowners realised the importance of lime on their land.

Bromyard Road in 1935, showing the first houses built for 'artisans' in Tenbury. There were no houses on the right hand side. The car is possibly that of a doctor on call.

The Pembroke Arms, 1905. This was bought by Pembroke College, Oxford as an investment in 1687 when the licensee was Philip Hill, alias Taylor. It was sold to the Godson family in 1889. This also had a toll-house in front of it, with two gates to the old road from the stepping stones. The foreground of the picture shows the large vegetable garden that existed but is now a car park. The beams on the right slope even more now. The Pembroke Arms has served both as a public house and as a farmhouse and when this picture was taken, was well known as a cider house.

The National School, 1905, in the Bromyard Road. This was built in 1855 by the architect, James Cranston, who was also responsible for the Round Market, the Corn Exchange, and the Pump Rooms. The boys had their playground on the left and the girls on the right; the new extension is on the left. The pipe-smoking men seem to be playing truant on what is now the Junior School's playing field.

Cornwall House, seen here in 1920, was built as a Dower House by the Cornwalls in the late eighteenth century. It contains some marvellous Georgian wall paintings in a shell alcove (see below). Walter Hewitt, a builder, was born and died eighty-three years later in this house. He took over the family business in 1904.

A nineteenth century wall painting, part of a series of paintings in a shell alcove in the lounge. They depict figures of the Georgian period and were probably painted when William Crundell owned the property. They may even be portraits of Crundell and his wife.

OPENING

of the Primitive

METHODIST NEW CHURCH,

TENBURY.

The opening SERMON will (D.V.) be preached, on

TUESDAY, MARCH 27th, 1894,

at 11 o'clock, by the

REV. G. MIDDLETON,

(Governor of Bourne College).

A SALE OF WORK

will be opened in the Old Chapel, at 12-30, by

MRS. W. C. CHUBB, of Ludlow,

to be continued the following day, commencing at Two
o'clock.   Admission by ticket :—

First Day, Sixpence.   Second Day, Threepence,

To be returned in Goods or Refreshments.

☞ REFRESHMENTS AT MODERATE CHARGES.

Instrumental and Vocal Music at intervals during the
afternoon.   A Cantata at 6 o'clock by Ludlow Choir.

ON SUNDAY, APRIL 1st,

Two SERMONS by the

REV. W. CLULOW.

Morning Service, 11 o'clock : Evening, 6-30.

A Cantata will be rendered by the Choir at 3 o'clock.

*Special Offerings at each Service in aid of
the Building Fund.*

Your Attendance and Hearty Co-operation will be esteemed a favour.

N.B.—Contributions, large or small, will be thankfully
received by any of the following members of the
Ladies' Committee.

Mrs. Joel Smith.   Mrs. David Gardner.
Mrs. Caleb Anthony.   Mrs. James Froggatt.
Mrs. James Swain.   Miss Fletcher.

Methodist New Church in 1894. The opening of the new church replaced a cottage fronting on to Cross Street. The old chapel (see next page) was renamed The Peoples' Hall and is still in use.

Methodist Old Church in 1890. Two cottages were bought and then pulled down to build this chapel in 1863. The chapel was of the Primitive Methodist persuasion. In 1874 the tumbledown cottage was pulled down and the ground ornamentally laid out to form a pretty approach to the chapel.

Lower Kyrewood in 1905. These farmhouses are off the beaten track but are probably near the site of a Priory of Cluniac Monks, endowed with lands and a water mill. Materials from the Priory were probably used to erect these old farmhouses.

A motor cyclist of 1920 whose Triumph 1919 with number plate AB 1971 appears to be his pride and joy.

The Cottage Hospital, seen here in 1905, was opened in December 1870 and all the expenses, including the purchase of instruments, during the first year were paid for by the foundress, Mrs Prescott.

The Cottage Hospital in 1915. After opening in December 1870 it was reported that the number of patients in the first year was thirty-nine, none of whom died.

The Cottage Hospital, photographed in 1971 to commemorate the centenary of the hospital. The gates and gardens were paid for by Mr Rollo in memory of his father and mother, who did much, including the provision of an operating theatre, to help the hospital.

The workhouse, Teme Street in 1920 in one of the few photographs taken in its working days. The entrance gates lead to the drive where the Clee Hill stone was dumped, to be broken up by the inmates in exchange for a night's lodging. The entrance to the Cattle Market was further up the street.

Workhouse inmates in 1920. A few of the workhouse inmates are enjoying the sunshine with the workhouse master and mistress, Mr and Mrs Kingston.

Three
Around the District

Tenbury, being a market town, is the main centre for trade for a wide surrounding area. These photographs attempt to cover this area.

The Swan and the Teme Bridge in 1904. The Swan Hotel, although in Burford, was the main hotel for Tenbury and most of the celebrities, such as G.B. Shaw, chose the Swan as their base. You can see the ribs on the arches on the Shropshire side of the bridge. These are part of the original mediaeval bridge. The cast iron sprigs between the arches are part of the 1867 widening. The gentleman on the left is fishing from the bridge, which is still a popular pastime.

The Swan Hotel in 1910 was generously covered in ivy; in fact, it had rather taken over. A well known sight were the yew trees on the left which were carved into 'fantastic shapes'. This was considered to be the main hotel in Tenbury and Anthony Trollope probably stayed here when he started to write his novel *The Warden* in 1852. He describes views across the river with a bend in it and seeing old men sitting on seats (see bottom of page 50). Although in his novel it was part of the cathedral, he could have seen men from the workhouse from the hotel. Trollope advised the Post Office and travelled around the district on horseback. In his autobiography he says that it was while in Tenbury that he started to write *The Warden*.

Motorcycles outside the Swan in 1920. The motorcycles appear to be a Singer, Hudson 1908, Bradbury, Triumph, ? and Sunbeam. The gentleman on the right is Mr Baverstock who was the clerk to the Godson estate. He lived in Stafford House.

Redditch MCC in 1913. The Stanford Bridge Hotel is the setting for this rally. Both machines in the foreground are V-Twin Royal Enfields, a make manufactured in Redditch at that time.

Station Bus in 1929. The Station Bus was a horse and carriage which belonged to the Swan Hotel and used to take passengers from the station. Here it is appearing in a Whit Monday carnival.

Robinson's cider works, c. 1950. At the rear of the Rose and Crown (middle left) can be seen the cider works with queues of tractors waiting to unload their cider apples.

Richard Lloyd's factory, seen here in 1951, started in Tenbury at the Crow Yard during the Second World War and then moved to this site in Burford. The railway line can be seen in the background. This was also the bed of the old canal. Carriages are waiting to be loaded at a siding on the left. The weighing machine cottage may be seen bottom left of the picture; there was a public weighing machine on the roadside and the brick hut is still there.

Steam train at Tenbury in 1956. The line from Wooferton to Tenbury was built in 1862 with the extension to Bewdley two years later. Seen here is the passenger train with engine No. 9717 on the 4:46 pm run to Ludlow.

The Rose and Crown in 1905; the pub is well covered in ivy. The buildings of Robinson's cider works can be seen over the roof top. Looking up Clee Hill Road the station entrance can be seen on the left. The pub sign at the side, of which only the frame remains, would have been used to attract passengers from the station.

The Rose and Crown in 1900 in an earlier picture of the pub without the ivy on the walls. This is the older part of the pub, dating back to the seventeenth century. Although it does not look it, the building is half-timbered. It is evident here that the roads were not in the best of condition. Rain soon turned them into a sea of mud and some became nearly impassable in the winter.

Tenbury Station in 1910 looking towards Wooferton. The engine is a 517 with four close-coupled carriages. The platform on the right-hand side was lengthened in 1911 and the gas lights were installed in 1909.

Tenbury Station in the same year as above but looking towards Bewdley. The signalman's house can be seen on the bridge. This was built for the canal which went on the same bed and was built in 1790. A large notice in the station drive proclaims: 'The Orchard Spa, Tenbury Saline Waters For Rheumatism and Gout'.

Railcar No.W32W for Wooferton Junction seen here at Newnham Bridge in 1961 in a view looking towards Wooferton. The station has been preserved and forms part of a nursery.

Railcar at Tenbury in 1956. The diesel railcar is heading for Ludlow. The line has only six more years to run before facing the 'Beeching' axe.

Station staff gathered together on the occasion of the retirement of the station-master, Mr Roberts, in August 1924. Back row: H. Gibbs, C. Jones, R. Martin, J. Pussey, Mr Holland, Mr Hardisty, E. Morris, N. Tipton, T. Lucas, C. Jones. Front row: F. Jones, Mr Foster, J. Morgan, Mr Roberts, Mr Bowers and two relief clerks. The signalman's cottage and garden can be seen at the rear.

Waiting for a train to Bewdley dressed to the 'height of fashion', 1905.

Little Hereford church in 1905. This is a Norman church with a massive defensive tower. The field in the foreground shows the remains of a deserted mediaeval village, of which the church was the centre.

Rectory Cottages, Little Hereford in 1905. By this time the building had been converted into three separate cottages but before 1870 it was just one rectory. The main part of the building is mid-sixteenth century and was known as a 'peculiar'; it was part of the living of the Chancellor of the Choir of Hereford Cathedral.

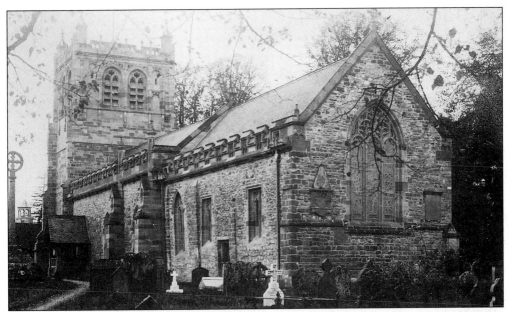

Burford church in 1905. Sir Aston Webb, architect and innovator in the Arts and Crafts Movement, renovated the church in the 1880s and the perpendicular influence is seen in the battlements. It has some fine monuments inside the church with the triptych being the most well known. There were some long-serving vicars in the area in the nineteenth century: Revd H. McLaughlin died in 1882 having served more than forty-five years; Revd Caleb Whitefoord died in 1890 having served more than forty-seven years and Revd Wayland Joyce, who died in 1887, served more than forty years.

Burford Rectory in 1905. Part of the house dates from the Tudor period (back left in the picture) but the front is from the 1880s when Sir Aston Webb renovated the church. All three incumbents of the portions of Burford (Burford, Boraston, Nash) originally lived at this rectory. Then, in about 1840, they had their own rectories built. The Revd C.G. Challenger was the last incumbent until it was run as St Mary's School by Revd. and Mrs Freeman.

The Duke of York in 1905. The Duke of York, Laysters, seems rather hidden away for a public house but in 1894 it was fully licensed, with a blacksmith's shop. It was sold at auction for £645.

The smallest cottage, c. 1900. A one-up and one-down residence in Middleton, a small hamlet to the north of Little Hereford, this cottage is now forgotten by even the oldest inhabitants.

Quarrying in 1905. This is a rather rare picture of men working one of the many local quarries. The stone is probably being used for repair work in a farmhouse or church. The 'tools' of the trade, including the cider bottle, can be seen scattered around.

Berrington Mill in 1905. The mill contained two pairs of stones driven by an 18 ft overshot water wheel which was powered by Cadmore Brook and gave up to 10 hp. The mill used the advertising slogan, 'Use Good English Flour made at Berrington Mill, And you will not want a Doctor or a Beecham Pill'.

Redwood House in 1960. In 1794 a huge maiden oak was felled at Redwood. Its girth was 5 ft 5 in, its length 46 ft and it weighed 27 tons. This remarkable tree was previously rented at two guineas per annum on account of it bearing mistletoe, which was celebrated for its virtue in curing fits and therefore sold at a good price.

Upton Oak in 1905. This oak was burnt down in 1850 by a fellow called 'Wild Will'. He was the terror of the countryside but was caught inside the hollow oak with a great deal of stolen spoil. He was tried at Hereford and sentenced to transportation. On his return he had his revenge on the oak by setting fire to it. It was forty-two feet round and over 1,000 years old.

The Cottage, Highwood, in 1925. Mrs Passey is seen here in front of her cottage. This was the last cottage to be thatched and when the thatch was removed, in about 1937, it was replaced by sheet iron and then painted with red oxide.

Kyre Post Office in 1905. This, like many others, has now gone as a post office. The cottage has been enlarged and 'modernised' and is hardly recognisable.

Burford House and church in 1936. The horticultural business of Treasures can be seen to be growing at the bottom of the picture. The River Teme runs across the picture while its tributary, the River Ledwych, can be seen joining it from the bottom right of the picture. Burford House was the home of the Cornewall family, the Barons of Burford. George Rushout had wings built onto the house in the 1860s but these have since been demolished. It is recorded that Mr James Lucas worked at Burford House for the Honourable Georgina Rushout from 1846 until her death in 1891. He had worked as a loyal sevant for forty-five years. He then retired to Ivy Villa, which he had been able to build himself, to enjoy his chief hobby of horticulture. He died, aged 84, in 1912.

Eardiston House in 1912. This is the rear of the house with the main Worcester road at the back. The owners, the Misses Wallace, used to invite school children to fêtes on the lawn and the food was spread out for them in the conservatory. The house is now divided into flats. Flossie, one of the maids, sent this card to her cousin in 1914 'to show where I live'.

The funeral of Miss Phoebe Wallace on 13 June 1946 leaving the gates of Eardiston House. The man leading the front horse is Richard Painter.

Eardiston Bridge linked Eardiston House with the farmlands over the main Tenbury to Worcester road. The bridge was cast in one piece in Stourbridge in 1827 and is now at Huddington Court, near Droitwich. The school children, when having parties at the house, used it to go and play games in the fields.

Abberley Hall, c. 1910. This is a little-seen view of the hall, now a school, that overlooks Witley Court. It was 'surrounded by a parcke on a mighty hyll, over-lookinge the paryshe of Abberley which lyethe underneathe in a botome'. The hall was built by the Moilliets in the 1840s after their purchase of the manor and is a fine building in the Italian style. Shortly after its completion in 1845, Moilliet died and fire destroyed the main part of the building on Christmas Day, 1845. In 1883 there was erected on Merritts Hill, the familiar Gothic style Clock Tower, which is a landmark for miles around. The parish boundary passes through Abberley Hall and the owner, Mr Jones, did not get on with the vicar of Abberley so, when he died, he ensured that he died in a room that was in the parish of Great Witley so that the burial service could be conducted in that parish.

Witley Court, *c.* 1910. This is a view of the Court in its heyday. It was burnt down in 1937 but is now in the care of English Heritage.

Great Witley, *c.* 1910. This view, probably taken from Abberley Tower with the Hundred House in the centre, shows Abberley Hill on the left and Witley Court in the distance on the right. The remains of what appears to be strip farming can be seen in the foreground. It was said that the Clock Tower was built so that the owner could look over the Foley estate of Witley Court.

St Michael's in 1920, was then a quiet country lane. The gate of Mrs Tombs' old post office can be seen on the left with the telephone sign on the tree on the right. The Gothic-style windows of the cottage are a fairly common sight in the area.

Oldwood Road, c. 1920. Mile End villas are on the left and the half-timbered house on the right was pulled down about thirty-five years ago for road widening, which is still awaited.

Talbot House in 1900. The people are on a day trip from the Talbot Inn, Newnham Bridge. The hotel has since been extended on the left but still in this rather ornate Gothic style. Three horses would be needed as there was quite a sharp hill on the road to Worcester or, even, the steamer at Holt Fleet.

Four
Rivers

The River Teme and its tributary, the Kyre, have been important in Tenbury's history, not only for the floods they caused in the town, but as important crossing places for traffic. As previously observed, it was said in 1615 that the bridge 'is the most important crossing for traffic between Wales and London'.

Teme Bridge in flood, 1901, on the downstream side of the bridge with Shropshire on the right. As can be seen this was a fairly major flood which caused a lot of stock damage in the cellars of the shops in Teme Street. The dangerous waters are attracting plenty of spectators.

The Swan Hotel and Teme Bridge, *c.* 1904. The fly fisherman is attracting quite a lot of attention. The Tenbury Fly Fishing Association was already sixty years old when this photograph was taken.

Opposite: Fishing Notice of 1817. The Tenbury Association for the preservation of game was formed by the local landowners to protect their own interests. The notice also included the canal which had been in use for about twenty-three years.

74

NOTICE

Respecting Fish.

WHEREAS, the Fish in the River Team, Leominster Canal, and other waters, have of late Years been much destroyed by Nets, laying Fish-Hooks and other Engines, which practices are contrary to Law,

Notice is hereby given,

That all Persons who shall use any Net, Angle, Hair-Noose, Troll, or Spear, or shall lay any Wears, Pots, Fish-Hooks, or other Engines, or shall take any Fish by any means or device whatsoever, or be aiding thereunto in the aforesaid River, or Water, or any other Waters, without the consent of the Lord or Owner of the Water, are liable, upon Conviction, to give to the party injured treble damages, and also to pay down to the *Overseers* for the use of the *Poor*, the sum of

TEN SHILLINGS

FOR EVERY SUCH OFFENCE.

And that such Damages and Penalty will in future be strictly enforced against every Offender, by the TENBURY Association for the Preservation of GAME; the Members whereof have caused this to be Printed for the information and caution of the Public.

Tenbury, September 9th. 1817.

Printed by B. HOME, Tenbury.

Tenbury Bridge in 1869. Major repair works were carried out fifty years after the Telford Bridge was built. Extra widening was given to the bridge by using the girder principle: corrugated iron was bolted together and finally several inches of reinforced concrete added. The notice says, sensibly, 'Dangerous'. This is a very early photograph of Tenbury and I would think that a ford had to be in operation while this repair work was taking place, probably where there is an existing walk down to the river.

Teme Bridge in 1905. This is the upstream side of the bridge and shows the county boundary between Shropshire on the north and Worcestershire on the south. The bridge is dated 1814 which is the date that Thomas Telford widened the bridge from its mediaeval width.

Dorothy's Rock, *c.* 1905. This is a small cliff on the Rochford side of Tenbury and is the spot where Dorothea, who lived in a cottage nearby, missed her footing and was drowned. The notice says 'No Fishing'.

Teme Bridge, *c.* 1908. Ice floes were a danger to the safety of the bridge and the Bridge Warden had to call for volunteers to help move them downstream if they started building up at the bridge. This was highly dangerous work in the middle of winter and the middle of the night. Notice the donkey and cart on the bridge. It could be that of 'Donkey Davies', the carrier from Rochford.

Skating in 1905. The pools seem to have frozen much harder in the early 1900s, so much so, that J.G. Banfield's used to sell skates. This photograph was probably taken on Kyre Pool. Skating was possible for two or three weeks and ice hockey was played.

Burford Weir in 1910. This was built by Lord Northwick to enable more parishioners to cross the river and attend Burford Church. It is about twelve feet wide although it has now collapsed in the middle. Note the ladder to climb the rock on the south side of the river.

Newnham Bridge. The bridge crossed the River Rea and has now been replaced by a much stronger looking bridge. The bridge shows up on Speed's map of 1650 so was obviously an important crossing place.

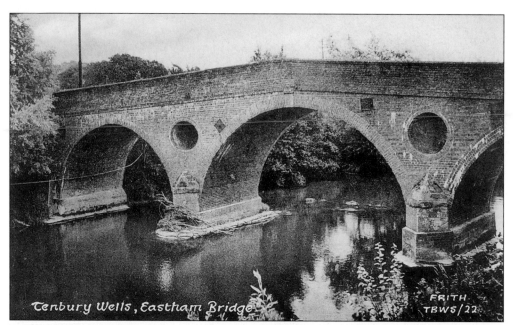

Eastham Bridge, c. 1930. This was built as a toll-bridge by E.V. Wheeler of Newnham Court and included a toll-house on the left hand side. During the Second World War a pillbox was built attached to the bridge.

Early car on Teme Bridge, c. 1920. The vehicle is either a Little Star or Britten, which were made in Wolverhampton.

William Norris, *c.* 1890. He came to Tenbury in 1849 as a solicitor and made a considerable impact on the town; he helped to found the railway, the Pump Rooms and the Volunteer Movement. He also helped to found the first National Schools in Tenbury and St Michael's College. His motto was 'I was taught as a boy to be useful to my fellow man, and I have tried to act on that principle'.

Meadows Mill Weir in 1950. This weir is on the Teme at Eardiston and was dismantled in 1960 to help save Tenbury being flooded. In 1896 there was a record catch of eels (5 cwt) at this weir, including a 6 lb silver eel.

Kyre Park Bridge in 1905: a pleasant looking bridge over the water system at Kyre Park Gardens. It has now been replaced by a wooden structure.

Boating on the Teme in 1905. This is at the Cliffs, Little Hereford. It was quite a sport to see who could row or paddle from Ludlow to Worcester in the fastest time. In 1894, two gentlemen from Oxford paddled upstream in seventeen and a half hours, returning in a time of nine hours.

Five
Sport and Recreation

Before the Second World War sport and recreation were mainly self-made: you made your own amusements and formed your own sporting clubs. A football club was formed when half-day closing was introduced. Before, the young shop assistants played by moonlight after the shops closed at seven in the evening. On one occasion in the early days of football in the town a ball burst and a horse had to be sent to Ludlow to collect another ball before the game could resume.

Cricket match at Penlu in 1920. Little appears to have changed. Perhaps the sight-screens are a bit more sophisticated. In 1891 the Tenbury captain, J.V. Wheeler, employed the services of a professional for ten weeks and beat Ludlow for the first time. Ludlow had their revenge by also employing a professional for the return match and beating Tenbury.

Tenbury Rugby Club, 1960. Although a hundred years old the club was reformed in 1958 and has flourished since then. Top row: M. Harrison, J. Hewitt, G. Morgan, I. Smith, M. Head, C. Bunn, A. Head. Second row: N. Faithful, R. Peak, J. Coles, R. Farr, J. Parton, D. Croxton, C. Adams. Front Row: C. Smith, J. Weston, R. Wood, D. Webster.

Cromwell Sports C.C. 1950. Richard Lloyd's cricket team were known as Cromwell Sports and were winners of the Orleton and District Cricket League which had just completed its first season. The team list is: G. Moss (Captain), G. Martin, G. Tanner, S. Nichols, E. Jones, W. Gardiner, J. Austin, P. Waterfield, E. Chell, G. Preece, D. Morris and P. Bates (Umpire).

Tenbury Cricket Team, 1908. Back row: J. Tearne, C. Partridge, J. Ashley, W. Thompson, B. Allen, A. Baldwin, W. Banfield. Front row: E. Thompson, R. Leake, W. Baldwin, W. Ashley (Captain), W. Rees, H. Hide.

Tenbury Hockey, 1933-34. Top left are L. Tudge, F. Lucas, P. Clifford, V. Tudge and on the bottom right is E.W. Faithfull.

Tenbury Hockey Team, 1913. The Tenbury Hockey Team, which then played on the Palmers, consisted of: J. Wormington, W. Ashley, J. Banfield, A. Gore, F. Roper, Godde, Leake, Robinson, Mace, E. Green, and F. Lucas.

Tenbury Hockey, 1910. When the two full backs 'Old Farf' Gore and Harry Higgins were playing the team did not lose for five years. It was said of their play that ' the ball was seldom on the ground but no one ever got killed'.

Tenbury Bowling Club, 1899. This was taken at a match with Hereford Bowling Club at The Swan Green. Back row: Mac White (vet), Downes (saddler), Yates (grocer), -?-, -?-, -?-, T. Adams (clothier), Edkins (tavern). Middle row: Rees, Rees (schoolmaster), Jarvis (surveyor), Pickering (bank manager), Wormington (baker), Hellaby (corn merchant), Pope (carpenter), Fuller (advertiser), Banfield (photographer), Higgins (workhouse master). Front row: -?-, -?-, -?-, -?-, -?-, -?-, Mattock (Royal Oak), -?-, -?-, -?-, Morris (chemist), Freeman (water bailiff). Lying down: Harry Higgins, Adams. It was said at the time that Tenbury could pride itself on its bowling club, largely due to the affable captain, S. Mattock. Any good club wishing to assess its strength was urged to take on Tenbury.

Bowls match at Burford, Gloucestershire in 1908. Lord Northwick arranged a bowls match between Tenbury and his estate workers at Northwick Park, near Burford, Gloucestershire. The Tenbury team was S. Mattock, R.C. Morris, J. Hellaby, T.H. Downes, G.H. Wormington, J. Davis, E. Hill, F.J. Bloom, E. Higgins, A.E. Smith, H. Wall, A.E. Walker, A.J. Edwards, C. Davies.

Tenbury Football, 1885. Although Association Football had only come to Tenbury three years before, there were three teams in Tenbury: St Mary's, Tenbury, with their captain, W. Hartland, Tenbury Silver Stars (captain, A. Webster), who played at the back of The Swan Hotel and Tenbury Institute, captained by Arthur Walker who gave the ground, goal posts, corner flags and football to the club.

Tenbury Football, 1891. Tenbury won the final tie against Leominster Runners by three goals to nil in the South Shropshire Challenge Cup. At 7:00 pm Tenbury were met at the railway station by the Tenbury Military Band and paraded through streets of Tenbury amidst a very enthusiastic reception. Team: -?-, S. Mills, -?-, -?-, E. Mills, Phillips, Baker, S. Hartland, W. Hartland, Round, -?-, F. Parkes.

Tenbury Thursdays Football Club, 1925. This soccer team was formed when half-day closing was introduced. They used to play in their own clothes and club together to buy the 10s ball. This photograph was taken at Ludlow, along the Bromfield Road, beside the munitions factory. The team played against Ludlow Thursdays, Leominster Thursdays and Ludlow Church Lads Brigade. The team only existed for about three years. Back row: Cyril Mitchell, Jack Wormington, Edward Banfield, Tapper Jones, Jim Banfield, George Bowkett, Billy Howles and Percy Jones. Front row: Cyril Cheese, Harry George, Nip Tipton, Charlie Davies and Tom Bloom.

Eastham Rangers, 1921. The team at their changing room of the Old Vicarage (now Robins End). They used to play on a field at Eastham called Nonsuch. The captain with the ball is Mr William Morris who is the present (1996) mayor's father.

Tug of war, 1928. Revd Chesterton umpires a tug of war between gents and ladies at the Palmers. The gentleman in charge of the ladies is an old Tenbury athlete, Charles Haywood.

Tennis party, 1905. A tennis party was a social occasion with time to show off your clothes as well as having the occasional match. Tenbury Tennis Club was formed in 1890 at The Swan with subscriptions of 5s.

Tennis at The Court in 1920. A fête was held at The Court grounds in aid of the new Tenbury Golf Pavilion. There were tennis tournaments and bowls competitions, accompanied by orchestral music. Admission was 1s for adults and 6d for children.

Cycling in 1905. Cycling was coming into its heyday as a recreational activity although ladies taking to the cycles caused some uproar, mainly over the matter of dress.

Ludlow, 1905. A favourite outing, made possible by the railway, was to Ludlow Castle. Here a group from Tenbury are posing in front of the fine Norman doorway.

Picnic, 1905. Having travelled by train to Church Stretton and then walked to Cardingmill Valley, it is time to settle down to a well-earned picnic.

Clee Hill Road, 1905. An outing, with carriage and pair, on its way to Clee Hill, perhaps for a bit of bird watching.

Camping, 1905. Camping was becoming a popular form of recreation, especially with the growth of the Boy Scout movement. It was not unusual for Tenbury youths to spend the whole summer camping out. It didn't cost anything, needing only the agreement of a friendly farmer.

Football at the Palmers in 1905. Football was a popular pastime played with a pig's bladder often after work had finished at 7:00 pm.

Pole vaulting, *c.* 1905. All recreation was home-produced. This gentleman might not have the style but the endeavour is there.

Swings in 1905, forever higher! It looks like a well-constructed swing with boarding underneath, but the greenhouse seems a bit close.

Tenbury Walk, 1965. The finish of the walk from Worcester to Tenbury was in the Cattle Yard. It was run by the Chamber of Trade with Eric Lowe, in the jockey's cap, as the chief organiser. The Chamber of Trade was formed in 1961 with Mr A. Gough as chairman.

St Mary's Bell Ringers, c. 1955. George Bowkett paid to have the old hand-bells renovated. The ringers are: Jean Claridge, Eric Lowe, David Lowe, Harold Ward, George Bowkett and Bruce Mytton.

Rifle range, 1905. The range was across the River Teme, firing from near the Castle Tump to the Butts, over the river in the flood plain. These butts can still be seen at the back of Cralves Mead.

Caravan, 1928. This caravan was built by G. Farmer for Revd Chesterton, Vicar of Tenbury.

Rifle range, 1900. This time it is the Tenbury Volunteers who are pictured. They held annual competitions and people donated prizes for the best shots.

Hunt at Kyre in 1905. This gives a good idea of how the great Kyre Deer Park would have looked with its famous oak trees. It is full of conifers now.

The Hunt in Church Street in 1913. The Ludlow Hounds are parading with John Jeff, a great hunt supporter, in the centre. Mr Jeff was Town Clerk for thirty years and was a keen member of the Tenbury Volunteers from its formation in 1859.

Maypole dancing, 1897. To celebrate the Diamond Jubilee the school children gave a display led by their headmaster, Mr Rees. One of the dancers was Miss Tipton who began her education at three, became a pupil teacher at 14 and taught at the same school until she was 66.

A meet of the Eastham Badger Club with the result of their day's work, 1900. Badgers were considered more as pests and needed to be controlled.

Charabanc outing, c. 1920. This was the first motorised charabanc outing organised from Tenbury. The coach is a Thornycroft or Vulcan and it will have had doors for each row of seats with a running board along the length. TBC Ltd. (Tenbury Bath Company) ran *The Queen of the Bluebirds* and used to run excursions to the races. In 1922 a trip went to the point-to-point at Eardisley Park; the return fare was 4s 6d.

Knowbury Bus, 1921. The Knowbury Bus Company ran this solid tyred bus, a Bristol, seen here as brand-new in 1921. It was named the *Green Parrot* and was finished in green and white.

Stanley Baldwin (with dog) canvassing for a general election, *c.* 1922. The party of supporters meet him on Newnham Bridge. The car is a 23/60 Vauxhall. Baldwin was Conservative MP for Bewdley and served as Prime Minister in 1923, from 1924 to 1929, and from 1935 to 1937, when he resigned, largely as a result of the Abdication Crisis.

The Swan Hotel, 1930. Shelsley Walsh personalities are on the steps of the hotel: Hans Stuck, (second from left, front row) and Rudolf Caracciola, (fourth from left, front row). Many of the racing personalities who attended the speed hill-climb stayed at The Swan.

Swan Hotel yard, 1936. Hans Stuck and Leslie Wilson, Secretary of the Midland Automobile Club, confer over the account of Shelsley in the paper in June 1936. Beside them in the yard of the Swan Hotel is Stuck's splendid Horch coupé.

Shelsley hill-climb, 1930. Hans Stuck is seen here in vivid action with his special Austro-Daimler at Shelsley Walsh. He broke the record for the hill-climb with a time of 42.8 seconds.

Angel Bank hill-climb, 1922. The Angel Bank, Clee Hill, was used for hill-climbing with the finish being near The Angel pub. Here, a sports Autocrat awaits the start and was timed over a half-mile course. The Longstone cottage in the background is still unchanged.

Tenbury Cricket Centenary, 1951. A match between Ancients and Moderns was played to celebrate 100 years of cricket in Tenbury. The Ancients were 114 all out and the Moderns, 117 for 5 wickets. The average age of the Ancients was 50. Ancients (above): H. Hingley, F. Worrall, C.L. Thorpe, A. Maund, L. Graves, R.W.K. Baker, H. Bentham, E. Dene, C.F. Parton, T. Quarterman, G. Coles, P. Jones. Moderns (below): H. Smith, C. Thatcher, J. Walsby, C. Howe, J. Coles, I.R. Barker, W. Fuszard, John Coles, A. Thorpe, Dr Burnett, R. Phillips, P. Fillery. Pip Jones took his 100th wicket of the season during the week's festivities.

Six
Special Occasions

Tenbury school children in 1898. Smocks seem to be the natural dress for both boys and girls at this time. This is a rather rare photograph of nineteenth-century local school children, names unknown.

Eastham School, Highwood, 1926. Back row: C. Morris, M. Newell, E. Thompson, M. Turner, M. Wall, M. Young. Middle row: D. Dark, L. Haines, Hooper, L. Ward. Front row: -?-, J. Froggatt, -?-, Smith, R. Meeks, W. Tetsall. The teachers are Miss F. Kings and Miss M. Yarnold.

Fancy dress, c. 1912. Taken at Goff's school, this is a photograph of a special occasion, judging by the shine on the boots. Among the characters are Jack and Jill, Bo Peep, Little Boy Blue, St George, Little Jack Horner and Red Riding Hood.

106

H.Tippins A.Muncaster A.Piget G.Bebb J.Dickinson L.Piget
J.Tippins E.Clare J.Ryder B.Griffiths J.Muncaster T.Muncaster
E.Tippins J.Barnise H.Cox H.Griffiths H.Muncaster F.Simmonds
A.Howells T.Barnise A.Oliver L.Ryder W.Weber G.Piter
J.Simmonds A.Ryder

NEVER ABSENT

St Michael's School, 1903. A picture of school children who were never absent from school during the year 1903.

Fancy dress in 1912, probably at the annual carnival. The jockey on the right has a poster 'National Health Insurance 7d'. Lloyd George introduced National Insurance in 1911.

The wedding, in 1925, of Mr and Mrs Edgar Ingram, taken in the yard of the Kings Head. The bride's father looks a bit self-conscious on his brick, but he is not the only one.

'Kyre Park Tenantry Dinner', 1931. This was held at The Swan Hotel. Mrs Baldwin-Childe had just died and the new owner of Kyre House, George T. Heath, gave the tenants a dinner to introduce himself. Mr Palmer of The Swan had decorated the tables with flowers, ferns and mosses. Motor-buses were engaged from Mr Critchley of Tenbury to take the tenants to and from Kyre. The dinner was arranged by the estate agent Mr E.T. Langford and the inmates of the Kyre Almshouses were not forgotten, as Mr Heath sent provisions to them. Mr Heath sold all the magnificent interior of Kyre House, including fireplaces, panelling, staircases and floorboards. In fact, everything that could be prised out of the house was sold by auction.

Opposite: 'Welcome Home Dinner', 1946. This was run by the British Legion to allow the people of Tenbury to express their thanks. Facing the camera are Bill Hopcutt, Jack Hill, Alec Earl and Dean Martin. The gentleman turning round is Justin Dipper.

Cutting the first sod in 1970. Committee members meet at the Palmers Meadow to cut the first sod for the Tenbury Swimming Pool. From left to right: G.R. Kendrick, F.E. Beaumont (farmer), J.D. Rogers (Clerk, Tenbury Town Council), V. Willson-Lloyd (Guild Treasurer), Dr J.E. Blundell-Williams, S.P. Thomas (Kyrewood House), Mrs M.D. Higginson, L. Ball

Kyre Park House, 1941. The house was opened as a Red Cross and convalescent home for 'other ranks' by the High Commissioner to South Africa. Here Lord Clarenden, the owner, is speaking with Stanley Baldwin, seated on the left studying his speech.

(Bedfords), A.W. Tudge (Chairman, Tenbury Town Council), E.G. Banfield, T.F. Higginson (Chairman, Tenbury Swimming Pool Guild), J. Greenwood (architect), H. Higgins, Mrs G.E. Blundell-Williams, Eric G. Lowe, Sgt. C. Young, J. McGrath (builder).

Tenbury school children in 1924. Boys: second from left, Eric Wallington, second from right, Ben Bowkett, third from right, Harold Middleton. Girls: Madge Badlan, Ida Lewis, Perkins, Fletcher, Phyllis Gregory, Mary Hulme, Annie Hulme, Wakeman, Monk, Mills.

Tenbury Home Guard, 1943. These are the Home Guards of Tenbury, Lindridge and Eardiston, Kyre and Stoke Bliss. Front row: -?-, E. Lowe, -?-, J. Higginson, O'Reilly, J. Knott, Bentham, Dr Williams, Guiness, R. Baker, Morgan, Selby, -?-. The two on the front left are Reece Davies and Sgt Viles. Second row: -?-, J. Pole, Mytton, Vobe, -?-, R. Robinson, -?-, Johnson, F. Vobe, -?-,

Coronation Parade, 1953. The carnival assembled in Bromyard Road and marched through colourful flag-decked streets, headed by a band of small children in fancy dress. They journeyed along Teme Street, over the bridge and to the hospital. Afterwards, they paraded in Palmers Meadow.

112

 G. Bowkett, L. Chambers, -?-, -?-, H. Davies, -?-. Third row: -?-, A. Allen, -?-, -?-, -?-, F. Pitt, -?-, -?-, -?-, C. Hartland, H. Wall, -?-, -?-, -?-, Canny Noble. On their third anniversary Brigadier General D'Arcy Legard said to them 'You will show the enemy that he has fallen, not into the poultry run, but into the lion's den'.

Young butcher in 1919. Six year old George Bowkett is being introduced to the butchery business outside Market Square. The firm is still going strong.

Boy Scout Band, *c.* 1913. Possibly St Michael's Boy Scout Band, they are dressed in the uniform that was worn prior to the First World War.

Tenbury 1st Volunteer Battalion, 1880. The battalion line up outside Tenbury Station for a church parade. Leading them is Captain Norris. Above their heads can be seen the Tenbury Bus, run by the Swan Hotel to ferry passengers to and from the station.

Seven
People at Work

As Tenbury is mainly an agricultural area, it is not surprising to see that most of the examples of people at work relate to the countryside.

The Cattle Market in 1920. This shows the horned cattle being auctioned off at the Thursday market. In these earlier days there were as many as 1,500 cattle sold in Tenbury market over a two day period. The chimney in the background belonged to the gasworks, across the river, together with the gasometer.

Two gardeners in 1920. Jim Turner, on the right, worked for Hewitt's the builder and is seen here, with a neighbour, at work on his vegetable patch next door to his cottage in Berrington Lane.

No 65 Teme Street in 1920. This is situated next to the Ship Hotel and Mrs Nott used to sell mainly sweets: 'a jelly for a penny'.

'Donkey Davies', 1920. He was a carrier from Rochford to Tenbury and used to deliver coal and groceries to people around Rochford. Each district had a carrier as these small and light carts could still travel the very muddy roads in winter when heavy carrier carts would get stuck in the mud.

Church worker, 1920. This is believed to be one of the Griffin family who devoted their life to keeping the church clean and functioning correctly. She is filling up with water at the vandal-proof tap. Fanny Griffin had a hard life and left her life story in dictated form. She was trapped in the 1886 floods in the Pump Room cottage where she survived for twenty-four hours on top of a chair on the bed and had to be rescued by boat.

H.M. Moore cutting grass for hay on a field at the side of Eastham Park Lane, 1930.

Rural postman in 1920. Here is one of Tenbury's rural postmen, Mr Cleeton, wearing their distinctive hat. The postmen had about a six-mile round, going out at 6:30 am and returning at 6:00 pm. There was a hut at the end of their round where they could rest and sell stamps and the like. Farmers used to give them drinks of cider on their rounds, so they could be quite drunk at the end. The people of Greete raised a subscription for their postman when he gave up drink.

Lower House Farm, Rochford, *c.* 1944. The Adams are seen here on their farm with two German POWs. Note the round trouser patch. From left to right: two German POWs, J. Adams, E. Powell, H. Adams.

Fruit shed, Newnham Bridge, *c.* 1930. G. Powell, with a horse and dray loaded with chips and sieves of fruit, is seen here at the fruit shed.

Cider-making in Tenbury in 1905. These travelling cider-makers used to go round the local farms to make cider. Here the complete process is being shown, from the pile of cider-apples in the rear to the rotary crusher, or scratter, on the right, then into the cheeses to be pressed and then, taken by the man with the yoke, to the barrels for natural fermentation. In 1885 it was said that 'cyder excites the appetite, clears the stomach, strengthens the digestion, frees the kidneys from gravel and bladder from stone. That made from pippins is an excellent remedy for consumption'.

Hop-pickers, *c.* 1930. The two children on the left were Betty and Kitty Cheese and the lady in the centre, in white, is Mrs Ingram. The cribs seem to have been individually made, some with more carpentry skill than others.

The Boat House, Eastham in 1927. Preparations are being made for a day's hop-picking. Hop-pickers: Mrs Moore, Cyril Moore, Mr Bennett and Bill Meeks.

Hopper's soup kitchen, 1918. This is a soup kitchen at Moor Farm. You can see the mangle for breaking up the vegetables and meat. The presence of a police constable seems to have been needed to ensure even distribution.

The midwife in 1920, Nurse Webber, is seen here going down Cross Street from her home in Berrington Lane.

The rear of the police station in 1954. This is now a doctor's surgery. You can see the police cells on the right. The notice says 'Witnesses Waiting Room'.

Police Sergeant Haynes, his wife and eleven children at the rear of the police station, 1890. Having spent eleven years at Tenbury making some very good arrests, Police Sergeant Haynes retired from the Force to take over the Colliers Arms.

Sam Dadge, 1920. Sam was a master farrier in Cross Street, where the vet's is now located. He had been Parish Clerk for over forty years, and, as shown here, he was a member of the Tenbury Fire Brigade, gaining a long-service medal and retiring with the position of Deputy Captain. He died in 1930.

Sam Dadge and his wife, 1920. Sam and his wife lived in a half-timbered row of cottages, now gone, in Berrington Lane. He is seen here at the bottom of his garden.

J.V. Parker, 1920, was a cabinet-maker working for Hewitts the builder and is seen here along the Bromyard Road. He was a strong supporter of the church and a member of its choir for many years.

Station-master, 1920. Here Mr Roberts, the genial station-master, is waiting to hand over the staff train key to the staff on the engine. He was the station-master for seventeen years until he retired in 1924. If he looked round he would see that King George V was about to board the train!

National Reserve, 1913. This was formed mainly from ex-serving soldiers and was led by Colonel Prescott of Bockleton Court. He is in the centre of the picture and flanked by two gentlemen with beards. On the left is Mr Pope and on the right, John Jeff, both of whom were long-service volunteers, having served since its formation in 1857.

Volunteers, 1867. The Tenbury Volunteers are on parade in Teme Street, with Captain Norris (second from left). Notice the background shops with the grand entrance to the Corn Exchange and on the left, what is now used as the Tourist Office in the summer. The Exchange House, on the right, was part of the Market Hall and is over 300 years old. It has been a grocer's, ironmonger's, house for Belgian refugees, United Services Club and British Legion Club. It became Tenbury's first supermarket.

Tenbury Rural District Council, 1956. Standing: J.E. Parkinson (surveyor), H. Bentham (Tenbury), J.T. Young (Pensax), I.C. Riley (Lindridge), Revd A.P. Randle (Knighton-on-Teme), Captain Astley Jones (Stockton), G.E.T.H. Maund (Tenbury), G.H. Cudby (Deputy Clerk), F. Lucas (late Clerk), Revd Walters (Lindridge), R. Bostock (Town Clerk). Seated: V. Moore (Tenbury), H. Brooks (Kyre), A. Lawrence (Stoke Bliss), H. Jones (Tenbury), J. Batley (Knighton-on-Teme), W.G. Maund (Chairman, Rochford), Admiral Tennett (Lord Lieutenant of Worcestershire), Miss Prescott (Bockleton), W. Morris (Stanford), E. Evans (Bayton), B. Davies (Mamble), Dr Blundell Williams (Tenbury).

Tenbury Station yard, 1920. A daily occurrence was the arrival of the horse and carts carrying milk-churns to catch the 7.30 am train to the Midlands and possibly Cadbury's chocolate factory. They went back to the farms with empty churns which the train brought back.

The headmaster of Tenbury School, Mr Long, is seen here with an assistant teacher, Norman Cox, outside the school entrance, 1920.